I am
Benjamin Franklin

BRAD MELTZER

illustrated by Christopher Eliopoulos

 ROCKY POND BOOKS

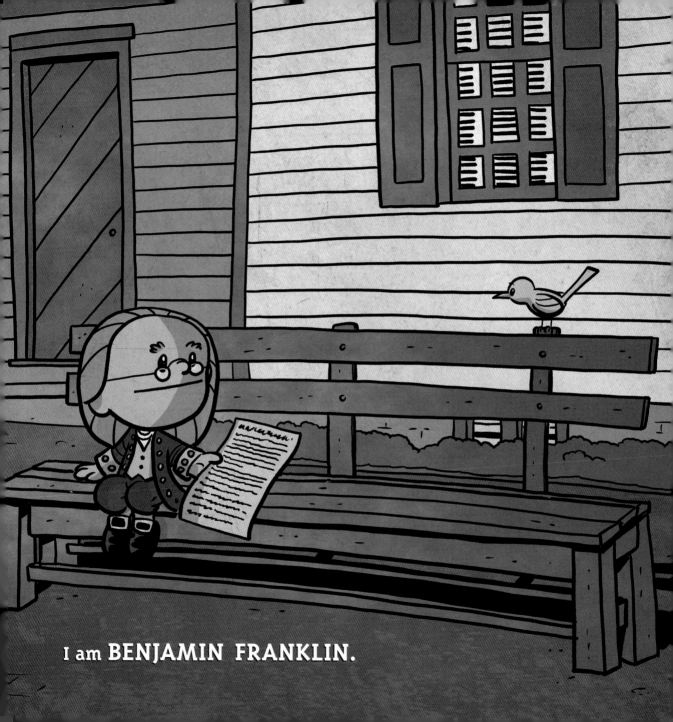

I am BENJAMIN FRANKLIN.

I come from a big family in Boston.
A *really* big one.
I was the youngest boy, with ten older siblings
and two younger sisters.

Floating on my back, I waited for it to pull me across the water.

If you're willing to experiment, you can learn something new—and use it to improve things.

At ten years old, I got my first job—working for my dad, making candles and soap.

Hoping to find something I liked, my dad showed me many different jobs.

I liked seeing all the ways to make things. The world has so much to discover. But there was one thing I liked most of all.

Reading books.
I loved reading so much that any time I had extra money, I'd use it to buy books.

That means history doesn't just happen by itself.
It's written—and built—and improved upon—by people like you and me.

Since I loved reading and writing, I went to work for my brother James.
He owned one of the most powerful tools in the world: a newspaper.
My brother's was the first independent paper in Boston.

I wanted to be a writer too, but my brother wouldn't let me.

So one night, when I was sixteen, I wrote an essay and slipped it under the door of the newspaper.

I used different handwriting and a fake name, pretending I was an old woman who lived in the countryside.

That's how I became a published author.

Eventually, I decided to forge my own path—to write my own history.

I headed for the big city...

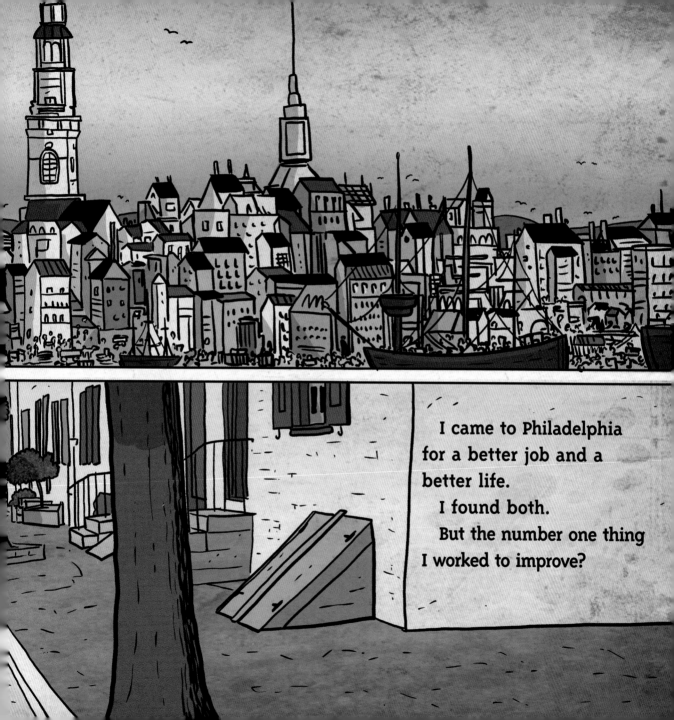

I came to Philadelphia for a better job and a better life.

I found both.

But the number one thing I worked to improve?

Myself.

In order to be a better person, I wrote new rules to live by, my very own "Plan for Future Conduct."

To sharpen my mind, I even started my own club—the Junto Club. We discussed the great questions of the day, like...

My most vital work came from my job. In Philadelphia, I opened a print shop for my own newspaper, the *Pennsylvania Gazette*.

I was a champion of the free press, printing many differing opinions.

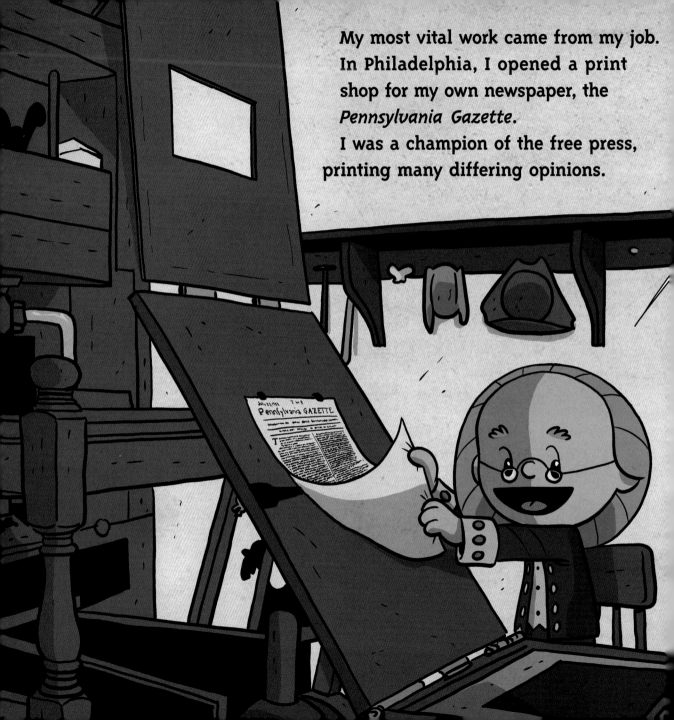

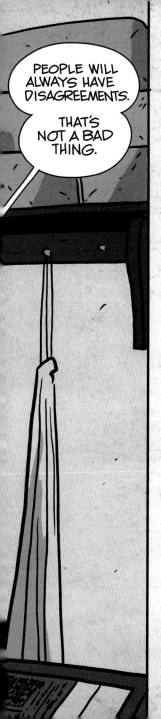

PEOPLE WILL ALWAYS HAVE DISAGREEMENTS.

THAT'S NOT A BAD THING.

Remember: If you listen to just one side of an argument, you won't have all the important facts. You won't be able to make an informed decision.

EARLY ON, BEN PRINTED THIS IMAGE, THE VERY FIRST POLITICAL CARTOON.

ITS MEANING WAS THAT WE'RE MUCH STRONGER WHEN WE STAND TOGETHER.

My real goal was to help my readers be better people.

If you want to improve the world, you need to start with yourself.

Over time, I made a newer and bigger list of virtues to follow in life: thirteen in total, including sincerity (which is meaning what you say), justice (which means treating people fairly), and humility (which means not bragging).

I tried mastering them all
at once, but it was impossible.

None of us is perfect.
But we can all keep working
to make ourselves better.

Throughout it all, I never lost my love of learning and discovery.
I observed how people got sick and became one of the first to figure out that colds are contagious.

I did experiments to prove how dark colors absorb more heat than light ones.

Electricity!

Back then, people didn't know exactly how electricity worked.

By observing it up close, I discovered that when there's a positive charge or energy of one type, there's also an equal negative charge, or energy that holds the opposite.

IT WAS A MASSIVE SCIENTIFIC BREAKTHROUGH.

First, I studied the problem.

I THINK IT'S THE METAL ON THE ROOF.

I THINK THE METAL IS DRAWING THE LIGHTNING FROM THE SKY.

At the time, I'd been waiting for a local church to finish building its steeple so we could put a metal rod up and test it.

They were taking so long that my son and I decided to try it ourselves. With a kite.

In June 1752, on a cloudy night, we put a pointy wire at the top of a silk kite.

Then we tied a key to the kite's wet string, hoping it would show us sparks after the lightning hit the wire.

ALMOST THERE.

ALMOST THERE...

And then...

LOOK AT THE STRING!

The strands started to rise.

People think I was an old man by then, but I was only forty-six and my son was twenty-one.

ALMOST THERE...

When the clouds first passed over...

NOTHING HAPPENED.

GIVE IT TIME.

ALMOST THERE...

AND THE KEY!

ZZT

IT WORKED!

INSTEAD OF HITTING AND BURNING THE KITE, THE LIGHTNING WAS ATTRACTED TO THE METAL.

Soon after, the world's very first lightning rods were installed in Philadelphia. To this day, rods around the world have prevented millions of fires.

Of all my experiments, perhaps the most *important* one was this: the American experiment.

Back then, the United States didn't exist yet.

There were no states—just thirteen colonies, all controlled by King George III, who was treating us unfairly.

Thomas Jefferson was selected to write a document that would declare our independence from England.

In it, we'd tell the king what kind of country we hoped to be.

People who lived here would have certain rights—to life, liberty, and the pursuit of happiness.

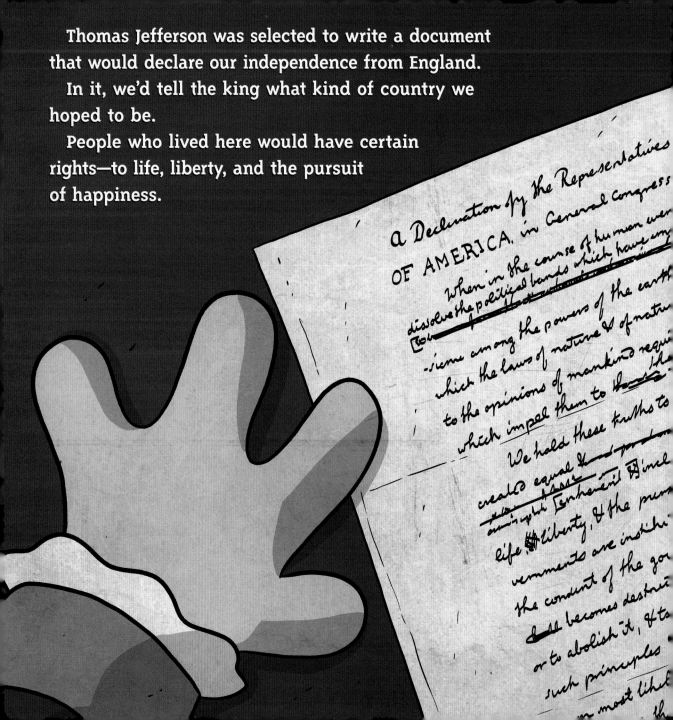

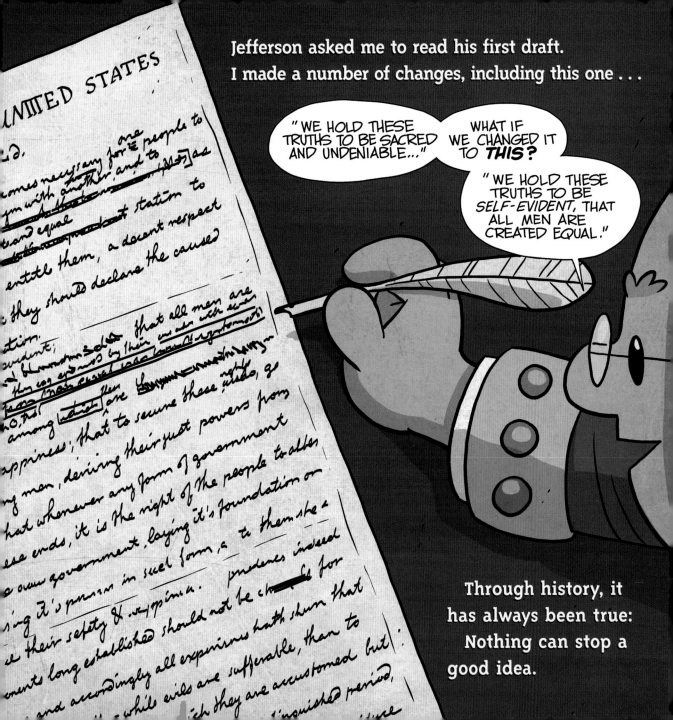

In my life, I worked hard to improve things—
including improving myself.
   That doesn't come easy.
   When you're trying to improve things,
there will always be a risk of failure.
   Don't let it stop you.
   By learning from failures, you will make progress.

New ideas are like lightning.
They can appear instantly, striking from
nowhere with staggering power.
That power is yours.
Use it wisely and...

I was a printer, a writer, an inventor, a scientist,
a scholar, and a Founding Father.
You don't have to be just one thing.
But you do need to be a good person.
You can always improve yourself.
You can always improve your world.

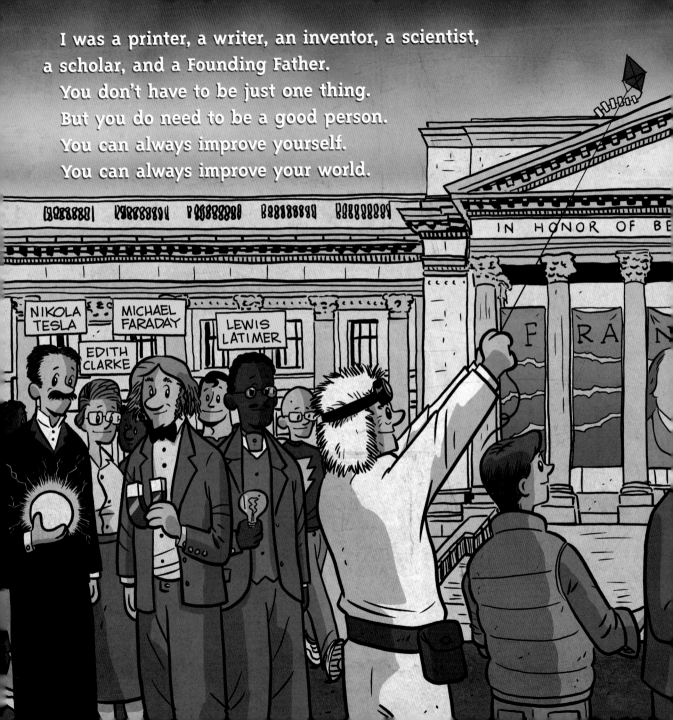

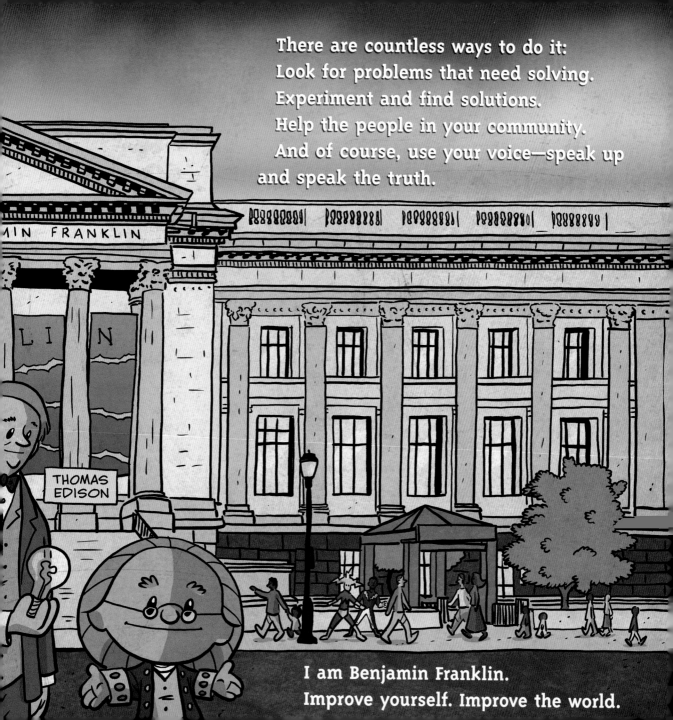

There are countless ways to do it:
Look for problems that need solving.
Experiment and find solutions.
Help the people in your community.
And of course, use your voice—speak up and speak the truth.

I am Benjamin Franklin.
Improve yourself. Improve the world.

"*Tell me and I forget. Teach me and I remember. Involve me and I learn.*"

—BENJAMIN FRANKLIN

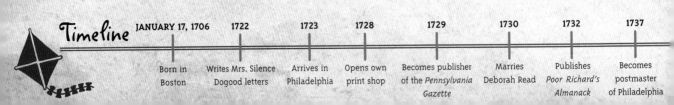

Timeline

JANUARY 17, 1706	1722	1723	1728	1729	1730	1732	1737
Born in Boston	Writes Mrs. Silence Dogood letters	Arrives in Philadelphia	Opens own print shop	Becomes publisher of the *Pennsylvania Gazette*	Marries Deborah Read	Publishes *Poor Richard's Almanack*	Becomes postmaster of Philadelphia

University of Pennsylvania

John Trumbull's painting
Declaration of Independence
(Yale University Art Gallery)

One of the faces
of American
currency

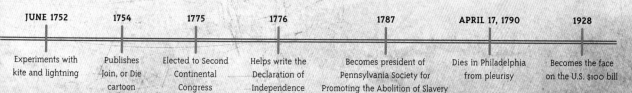

JUNE 1752	1754	1775	1776	1787	APRIL 17, 1790	1928
Experiments with kite and lightning	Publishes Join, or Die cartoon	Elected to Second Continental Congress	Helps write the Declaration of Independence	Becomes president of Pennsylvania Society for Promoting the Abolition of Slavery	Dies in Philadelphia from pleurisy	Becomes the face on the U.S. $100 bill

For Ami and Matt Kuttler,
who have always helped me be my better self.
And for Ryan, Ali, and Benny,
I take so much pride in being your uncle.
Keep chasing your passions—
I'll be cheering.
—B.M.

For Ken Lopez,
who got me started in my career
and my life.
—C.E.

For historical accuracy, we used Ben Franklin's actual dialogue whenever possible.
For more of Mr. Franklin's true voice, we recommend and acknowledge the below titles.

Special thanks to Susannah Carroll and our friends at The Franklin Institute, located
in Philadelphia, Pennsylvania, for their input on early drafts.

· ·

SOURCES

The Autobiography and Other Writings by Benjamin Franklin (Signet, 2014)
Benjamin Franklin: An American Life by Walter Isaacson (Simon & Schuster, 2003)
Benjamin Franklin by Edmund S. Morgan (Yale Nota Bene, 2003)
The date of Franklin's kite and key experiment comes from a later recounting
by Joseph Priestley, which can be read on Founders Online courtesy of the National Archives:
https://founders.archives.gov/documents/Franklin/01-04-02-0135

FURTHER READING FOR KIDS

Electric Ben by Robert Byrd (Dial, 2012)
Now & Ben by Gene Barretta (Square Fish, 2008)
Who Was Ben Franklin? by Dennis Brindell Fradin (Penguin Workshop, 2002)

· ·

ROCKY POND BOOKS
An imprint of Penguin Random House LLC, New York

First published in the United States of America by Dial Books for Young Readers, an imprint of Penguin Random House LLC, 2020
This edition published by Rocky Pond Books, an imprint of Penguin Random House LLC, 2023

Text copyright © 2020 by Forty-four Steps, Inc. • Illustrations copyright © 2020 by Christopher Eliopoulos

Rocky Pond Books & colophon are trademarks of Penguin Random House LLC. • The Penguin colophon is a registered trademark of Penguin Books Limited.

Visit us online at penguinrandomhouse.com.

Library of Congress Cataloging-in-Publication Data is available.

Portrait on page 38 by John Duplessis, courtesy of the National Portrait Gallery, Smithsonian Institution; gift of the Morris and Gwendolyn Cafritz Foundation
Photo of statue on page 39 courtesy of John Greim/LightRocket via Getty Images

Manufactured in China on acid-free paper • ISBN 9780525555919 • 10 9 8 7
Designed by Jason Henry • Text set in Triplex • The artwork for this book was created digitally.

The publisher does not have any control over and does not assume any responsibility for author or third-party websites or their content.